First World War
and Army of Occupation
War Diary
France, Belgium and Germany

60 DIVISION
179 Infantry Brigade,
Brigade Machine Gun Company
27 March 1916 - 1 December 1916

WO95/3030/7

The Naval & Military Press Ltd
www.nmarchive.com
Published in association with The National Archives

Published by

The Naval & Military Press Ltd

Unit 10 Ridgewood Industrial Park,
Uckfield, East Sussex,
TN22 5QE England
Tel: +44 (0) 1825 749494

www.naval-military-press.com
www.nmarchive.com

This diary has been reprinted in facsimile from the original. Any imperfections are inevitably reproduced and the quality may fall short of modern type and cartographic standards.

© Crown Copyright
Images reproduced by permission of The National Archives, London, England, 2015.

Contents

Document type	Place/Title	Date From	Date To
Heading	WO95/3030/7		
Heading	60th Division 179th Infy Bde 179th Machine Gun Coy. Jun-Nov 1916		
Heading	War Diary Of 179 Machine Gun Company. From June 25th., 1916. To 31st., July 1916 Volume No. 1.		
War Diary	Grantham	27/03/1916	25/06/1916
War Diary	Southampton	26/06/1916	26/06/1916
War Diary	Le Havre	27/06/1916	29/06/1916
War Diary	Tincques	29/06/1916	29/06/1916
War Diary	Penin	29/06/1916	30/06/1916
War Diary	Acq	01/07/1916	02/07/1916
War Diary	Trenches	03/07/1916	08/07/1916
War Diary	Acq	09/07/1916	12/07/1916
War Diary	Trenches	13/07/1916	29/08/1916
Heading	War Diary 179 Machine Gun Company September 1916 Vol 4		
War Diary	Trenches (Trench Map Roclincourt 51B-N.W.1 Edition 2 C Scale 1:10,000)	30/08/1916	29/09/1916
Heading	War Diary Of 179th Machine Gun Company From 1st October 1916 To 31st October 1916 Vol 5		
War Diary	Trenches (Roclincourt Map N.W.1 51B-Edition 2 C Scale 1/10,000)	29/09/1916	29/10/1916
War Diary	Ribeaucourt	30/10/1916	31/10/1916
Heading	War Diary Of 179th Machine Gun Co For November 1st-30th 1916 Vol 6		
War Diary	Ribeaucourt	01/11/1916	03/11/1916
War Diary	Vauchelles-Les-Quesnoy	04/11/1916	17/11/1916
War Diary	In Train	18/11/1916	20/11/1916
War Diary	Camp	21/11/1916	22/11/1916
War Diary	In Camp Of Marseilles	23/11/1916	25/11/1916
War Diary	At Sea	26/11/1916	01/12/1916

WO 95/3030/7

60TH DIVISION
179TH INFY BDE

179TH MACHINE GUN COY.

JUN - NOV 1916

CONFIDENTIAL

War Diary

of

179 Machine Gun Company.

from June 25th., 1916.   to   31st., July 1916

Volume No. 1.

Army Form C.2118.

WAR DIARY
INTELLIGENCE SUMMARY
(Erase heading not required.)

Instructions regarding War Diaries and Intelligence Summaries are contained in F.S. Regs., Part II. and the Staff Manual respectively. Title Pages will be prepared in manuscript.

Place	Date	Hour	Summary of Events and Information	Remarks and references to Appendices
GRANTHAM	27-3-16	—	Formation of Company, Entitled 179 Machine Gun Company.	R.J.R.
"	25-6-16	10:30 p.m.	Company Entrains for the Front.	R.J.R.
"	"	11:30 p.m.	Company leaves GRANTHAM military Dock	R.J.R.
SOUTHAMPTON	26-6-16	7:30 a.m.	Train arrives SOUTHAMPTON Dock	
"	"	7:30 a.m. – 9 a.m.	Unloading men, animals, limbers & baggage from train & placing same on S.S. Queen of Benares City	R.J.R.
"	"	6:30 p.m.	Ship leaves SOUTHAMPTON	
LE HAVRE	27-6-16	6 a.m.	Arrival outside LE HAVRE	
"	"	8:30 a.m. – 1:30 p.m.	Disembarkation. Stores indented for and drawn.	R.J.R.
"	"	3 p.m.	March off from Docks.	
"	"	3:30 p.m.	Reach Rest Camp	
"	28-6-16	9 a.m.	Company parades for cleaning guns & fitting Dicection Dials & Elevating Dials.	
"	"	11 a.m.	Medical Inspection: Two men sent to Hospital with Scabies.	R.J.R.
"	"	11 p.m.	March off from Rest Camp.	

Army Form C. 2118.

WAR DIARY

~~INTELLIGENCE SUMMARY~~

(Erase heading not required.)

Instructions regarding War Diaries and Intelligence Summaries are contained in F.S. Regs., Part II. and the Staff Manual respectively. Title Pages will be prepared in manuscript.

Place	Date	Hour	Summary of Events and Information	Remarks and references to Appendices
LE HAVRE	28-6-16	12.5 mid-night	Company arrives at GARE des MARCHANDISES	
		12.5 a.m. – 1 a.m.	Entraining:– men 25 to a cattle truck. Officers 3 to a 2nd Class compartment. Horses & mules, 8 to a truck & parallel to length of truck facing inwards in two lots of 4 each — secured by head ropes to rings in roof, breast rope in front of each lot & 2 men sleeping in centre. Two limbered wagons to an open Truck. Rations and forage in one truck. R.J.R.	
	29-6-16	2.59 a.m.	Train leaves GARE des MARCHANDISES & travels to TINCQUES, via ROUEN, ABBEVILLE & ST. POL.	
TINCQUES	"	9 p.m.	Arrival at TINCQUES and detrainment.	
"	"	10 p.m.	March off from station.	
PÉNIN	"	12 m.n.	Arrival at Farm DOFFINE near PÉNIN. Billets occupied & limbers(parks) — R.J.R.	
	30-6-16	—	Ordinary Parades. — R.J.R.	
ACQ	1-7-16	10.30 a.m.	March from Farm DOFFINE proceeding via SAVY, AUBIGNY, CAPELLE FREMONT and FRENIN CAPELLE to ACQ. R.J.R.	

Army Form C.2118.

WAR DIARY
INTELLIGENCE SUMMARY
(Erase heading not required.)

Instructions regarding War Diaries and Intelligence Summaries are contained in F.S. Regs., Part II. and the Staff Manual respectively. Title Pages will be prepared in manuscript.

Place	Date	Hour	Summary of Events and Information	Remarks and references to Appendices
ACQ	1-7-16	1:30 p.m.	Arrival at ACQ – men billeted in large Company Hut. — R.J.R.	
	2-7-16	12 noon	Parade of ½ Company with rest, guns to proceed to Trenches in ROLLINCOURT Sector. One officer, two N.C.O's & ½ of each 4 Gun Teams from each Section to be attached to 153 Bde. M.G. Coy for instruction. March off through ECOIVRES & MOULIN du BRAY. Met at MOULIN du BRAY by guides for whole Company. Proceed up towards "Territorial" Trench in groups of not more than fives at 25 yards distance; during last ¼ mile before entering "Territorial" Trench distance of 100 yards between groups kept. On entering "Territorial" Trench whole ½ Coy gathered together again & proceed forward in single file with officer & guide in front & a Senior N.C.O. in rear of whole ½ Coy to check stragglers. On reaching end of "Territorial" Trench met by guides from each Gun Team of 153 M.G.C., who took each ½ Gun Team of 179 M.G.C. to its position. Line occupied by 153 M.G.C. approximately A4 c09 99 to A16 c16 82, reserve Trench Map ROLLINCOURT (51ᵇ N.W.1 Edition 2.B. Scale 1:10,000) — R.J.R.	

Army Form C. 2118.

WAR DIARY
INTELLIGENCE SUMMARY
(Erase heading not required.)

Instructions regarding War Diaries and Intelligence Summaries are contained in F.S. Regs., Part II. and the Staff Manual respectively. Title Pages will be prepared in manuscript.

Place	Date	Hour	Summary of Events and Information	Remarks and references to Appendices
Trenches	3-7-16		Half Gun Teams of 179 M.G. Coy. Took over all duties of Gun Teams to which attached:- Snipping Post, Ration parties, working parties, etc. Quiet Generally. — Man of No 4 Section Killed by bullet in chest — R.J.R.	
"	4-7-16		Usual Trench Routine; nothing to report — R.J.R.	
"	5-7-16	3.30 p.m	Relief of ½ Coy. 179 M.G.C. by other ½ Coy of 179 M.G.C. — The latter ½ for two sections R.J.R.	
"	6-7-16	—	Usual Trench Routine for ½ Coy in Trenches. Other ½ Coy Carry on with ordinary parades. R.J.R.	
"	7-7-16	—	" do " R.J.R.	
"	8-7-16	—	Latter ½ Coy of 179 M.G.C. came out of Trenches. R.J.R.	
ACQ	9-7-16	9.30	Church Parade. R.J.R.	
	10-7-16	—	Ordinary Company Parades. R.J.R.	
	11-7-16	—	" do " R.J.R.	
	"	6.30 p.m	Nos. 1 & 4 Sections march off from ACQ with Limbers. At MAROEUIL Guns, etc. entrained from limbers on to Trucks to MAISON BLANCHE, where guns, etc. entrained & returns through up. Men proceed via Territorial Trench to MAISON BLANCHE. Night spent at MAISON BLANCHE. R.J.R.	

2449 Wt. W14957/M90 750,000 1/16 J.B.C. & A. Forms/C.2118/12.

Army Form C.2118.

WAR DIARY
INTELLIGENCE SUMMARY
(Erase heading not required.)

Instructions regarding War Diaries and Intelligence Summaries are contained in F. S. Regs., Part II. and the Staff Manual respectively. Title Pages will be prepared in manuscript.

Place	Date	Hour	Summary of Events and Information	Remarks and references to Appendices
	12-7-16	6 a.m.	Nos 1 & 4 Sections proceed to their positions led by guides from 153 M.G.C. & relieve Nos 1 & 4 Sections of 153 M.G.C.	
	"	6.30 p.m.	Nos 2 & 3 Sections of 174 M.G.C. proceed from A.C.Q. to MAROEUIL with limbers, then head on to Bailleys Plane same procedure as in case of Nos 1 & 4 Sections — their head me to Bailleys Plane Same procedure as in case of Nos 1 & 4 Sections	R.J.R.
Trenches	13-7-16	6 a.m.	Guides for Nos 2 & 3 Sections move off with guns, etc & relieve 2 & 3 Sections of 153 M.G.C.	
		12 noon	Relief of 153 M.G.C. complete. Line held that of 174th Inf. Bde. N. Sector with heads Qrs O & M Sectors ROCLINCOURT Sector.	R.J.R.
	14-7-16	—	Very quiet day. Disposition of guns as taken over from 153 M.G.C. :— 3 guns in front line Trench, 8 guns in support line, 4 guns behind support line (approx. 1400ᵡ from our own front line Trench for overhead firing) One gun in reserve. R.J.R.	

Army Form C.2118.

WAR DIARY
INTELLIGENCE SUMMARY
(Erase heading not required.)

Instructions regarding War Diaries and Intelligence Summaries are contained in F.S. Regs., Part II. and the Staff Manual respectively. Title Pages will be prepared in manuscript.

Place	Date	Hour	Summary of Events and Information	Remarks and references to Appendices
Trenches (ROCLINCOURT sector)	15-7-16		Rear Hqrs. Ad. Qrs. established at BRAY, about 2/3 mile S.E. of ECOIVRES (ref. LENS.11. Scale 1:100,000.)	
"	"	9:30 p.m. – 10:30 p.m.	The following points were identified with indirect fire. Enemy Trenches near A11 a.1.6, Road near A17a 5.2. Cross Roads in LES TILLEULS & Anopheles German Ht. Qrs A17 d.1.6. Reference ROCLINCOURT (51.b.N.W.1 Edition 2.B. Scale 1:10,000) – R.Q.R.	R.Q.R.
"	16-7-16	10 p.m. – 11 p.m.	Indirect fire by our M. Guns on various points in Enemy lines, suspected dumps, etc. – R.Q.R.	R.Q.R.
"	17-7-16	–	Our 3 guns withdrawn from front line Trench & positions taken over by Lewis Guns. Our 3 guns withdrawn placed in Reserve, thus making 4 guns in reserve. Three sections are kept in Trenches & one section armed down the hillside for rest. This arrangement of 3 sections in & one out is to be adopted for the future.	
"	"	9:45 p.m. – 10:15 p.m.	Our Vickers Guns continued to harry Enemy & search his lines. – R.Q.R.	R.Q.R.

Army Form C. 2118.

WAR DIARY
or
INTELLIGENCE SUMMARY
(Erase heading not required.)

Instructions regarding War Diaries and Intelligence Summaries are contained in F. S. Regs., Part II. and the Staff Manual respectively. Title Pages will be prepared in manuscript.

Place	Date	Hour	Summary of Events and Information	Remarks and references to Appendices
Trenches				
ROCLINCOURT (Sector)	18-7-16		Enemy very quiet.	
		10-11 p.m.	Indirect fire by our guns was brought to bear on several points in hostile area	R.I.R.
"	19-7-16		Comparative quiet	
		10.30 – 11.30 p.m.	Indirect searching fire by our overhead guns	R.I.R.
"	20-7-16		Enemy Trench Mortars very active in afternoon one of our guns at A.1.6.a.08.08 (ref. ROCLINCOURT Sector) being buried, but was undamaged	R.I.R.
"	21-7-16	10.10 p.m. – 10.50 p.m.	Indirect fire by our overhead guns	R.I.R.
"	22-7-16		Nothing to report. Usual Trench Routine	R.I.R.
"	23-7-16			

WAR DIARY or INTELLIGENCE SUMMARY

Army Form C. 2118.

Instructions regarding War Diaries and Intelligence Summaries are contained in F. S. Regs., Part II. and the Staff Manual respectively. Title Pages will be prepared in manuscript.

(Erase heading not required.)

Place	Date	Hour	Summary of Events and Information	Remarks and references to Appendices
Trenches ROCLINCOURT (Sector)	24-7-16		The muzzle-cap of one of our guns while firing worked loose. The muzzle-cap turned round, so that the clamping screw came on top. This had the effect of preventing the winding portions giving sufficiently far back for the hammer of the extractor to engage in the steps of the solid cam. The result was that the working portions flew forward & the top cartridge on the face of the extractor exploded the # cartridge which had been fed up into the face of the feed-block. The feed-block was quite undamaged. R.J.R.	
"	24-7-16	10-10.30 p.m.	Our overhead guns carried out Indirect searching fire on enemy lines.— 16 R.C.O's from 4 Battalions in Brigade attached to Company as gunners.	R.J.R.
"	25-7-16	—	Fairly quiet day. — R.J.R.	
"	26-7-16	10-11 p.m. 5 p.m.	1250 rounds fired by, Mr. M. Guns overhead indirect. No 1 Section advised No 3 Section	R.J.R.

Army Form C. 2118.

WAR DIARY
~~INTELLIGENCE SUMMARY~~
(Erase heading not required.)

Instructions regarding War Diaries and Intelligence Summaries are contained in F. S. Regs., Part II. and the Staff Manual respectively. Title Pages will be prepared in manuscript.

Place	Date	Hour	Summary of Events and Information	Remarks and references to Appendices
TRENCHES (ROCLINCOURT Sector)	27-7-16	—	Nothing to report. Usual Trench Routine — R.J.R.	
"	28-7-16	9·15 p.m	Our Engineers exploded a mine on our Left. Slight Bombardment — R.J.R.	
"	29-7-16	5·30 p.m	No 3 Section Wilson No 4 Section Indirect fire was employed on Paths & Dumps in Enemy Lines — R.J.R.	
		10-11 p.m		
"	30-7-16	—	Nothing to Chronicle — R.J.R.	
"	31-7-16	9·30 p.m	Indirect fire was brought to bear on Cross Roads in Enemy lines 1250 rounds being expended — R.J.R.	
		12.m.n		

Army Form C.2118.

WAR DIARY
or
INTELLIGENCE SUMMARY

(Erase heading not required.)

Instructions regarding War Diaries and Intelligence Summaries are contained in F. S. Regs., Part II. and the Staff Manual respectively. Title Pages will be prepared in manuscript.

Place	Date	Hour	Summary of Events and Information	Remarks and references to Appendices

2449 Wt. W14957/M90 750,000 1/16 J.B.C. & A. Forms/C.2118/12.

Army Form C. 2118.

August 1916

179th M.G. Coy

Vol II

WAR DIARY
INTELLIGENCE SUMMARY
(Erase heading not required.)

Instructions regarding War Diaries and Intelligence Summaries are contained in F.S. Regs., Part II. and the Staff Manual respectively. Title Pages will be prepared in manuscript.

Place	Date	Hour	Summary of Events and Information	Remarks and references to Appendices
Trenches ROCLINCOURT Sector.	1-8-16		Day fairly quiet. Enemy shelled ravine left about mid-day causing damage near A4.c.39.28 also near A4.c.09.09. It is thought that they were searching for a M.G. gun which the Brigade on our left bring to the ravine next to our gun at A4.c.09.99.	
TRENCH MAP ROCLINCOURT 51B N.W.1. Section 2c (Scale 1:10,000)	"	10 p.m. – 11 p.m.	Got an officer's dug-out at A10.a.20.60 & also from the Lewis Gunner's dug-out. Unknown crews hopping has been heard. This period is 500x from Enemy's lines.	R.J.R. (1-8-16)
			Indirect fire was brought to bear by 2 of our guns on fixed points of another point behind Enemy lines	R.J.R. (1-8-16)
"	2-8-16		Quiet day: Aerial activity in depth cross:	
		10.30 p.m – 12.30 a.m.	Enemy M.G. guns were active at night. 2,000 rounds expended by our M.G. guns in indirect fire on following Targets:– Suspected Dump at A5.d.20.60 & German Wire at A1.b.80.60 and dug-out near Cerkelsberg - R.J.R. (2-8-16)	
"	3-8-16		In the morning there was considerable Trench mortar activity in area from A4.c.09.99 to A10.a.61.45. About 16 of our aeroplanes passed over in direction of German lines at 12.45 p.m. returning between 1 & 1.30 p.m.	
"	"	10.15 p.m – 11 p.m.	Indirect fire brought to bear on Enemy Trenches near A5.a.30.40 also in Road from Am.6.0 to A1.a.45.45. Machine gun broken after firing about 250 rounds –	R.J.R. (3-8-16)

② August 1916

WAR DIARY
—or—
INTELLIGENCE SUMMARY
(Erase heading not required.)

Army Form C. 2118.

Instructions regarding War Diaries and Intelligence Summaries are contained in F. S. Regs., Part II. and the Staff Manual respectively. Title Pages will be prepared in manuscript.

Place	Date	Hour	Summary of Events and Information	Remarks and references to Appendices
Trenches (ROLLINCOURT) 51.B. N.W. Edition 2C Scale 1:10,000	4-8-16		On the whole a quiet day. A number of our aeroplanes passed over our lines between 6 p.m. & 9 p.m. They were heavily bombarded by enemy anti-aircraft guns & were compelled to turn back each time on reaching the German lines. A machine gun, not noticed before, was enfilading one of our communication trenches on the left hand sector of the Brigade front.	
"	"	10.15 p.m. – 10.35 p.m.	Indirect fire brought to bear by two of our guns on following targets:— 1. Road near B.M. 95.7. A.17.a.25. Range 2400" 2. Light Railway near A.17 & 30.45 Range 2000"	R.J.R. (4-8-16)
"	5-8-16	10 p.m. – 11 p.m.	Exceptionally quiet day. A few enemy trench mortars fell near a M.G. emplacement in right hand sector of Brigade front—no damage done. Our overhead guns employed indirect fire on Ecurie Roads & Ridges in Roclincourt area.	R.J.R. (5-8-16)

2449 Wt. W14957/M90 750,000 1/16 J.B.C. & A. Forms/C.2118/12.

(B) August 1916

WAR DIARY
or
INTELLIGENCE SUMMARY
(Erase heading not required.)

Army Form C. 2118.

Place	Date	Hour	Summary of Events and Information	Remarks and references to Appendices
Munches (ROCLINCOURT) 51.B.N.W.1 Edition 2C (Scale 1:10,000)	6-6-16	10 p.m. – 10.50 p.m.	Another fairly quiet day. Nothing of importance to chronicle. Two of our overhead guns employed indirect fire on bases known & suspected Dump behind Enemy lines. It has been noticed during the firing of our guns that the quality of the ammunition in many instances is quite inferior to M.G. used. Ammunition marked "N.S" & "L" is uniformly of poor quality causing a lot of stoppages (especially separated cases). Some of the rounds have abnormally thick rims & have in consequence a very damaging effect on the grooves of the extractor. Ammunition marked "L" has also given a good deal of trouble. Ammunition marked "K" (from experience to date) is the most satisfactory for M.G. uses. — — — — — R.J.R. (6-6-16)	

August 1916

WAR DIARY
INTELLIGENCE SUMMARY

(Erase heading not required.)

Army Form C. 2118.

Place	Date	Hour	Summary of Events and Information	Remarks and references to Appendices
Trenches (Roclincourt) 51 D.N.W. Edition 2C Scale 1:10,000	7-5-16	10 p.m.	Indirect fire by two of our guns on THELUS + Cross Roads. Silent Enemy lines.	
		~10 p.m.	Artillery activity on both sides — R.J.R.	
	8-5-16	—	Nothing of importance to chronicle. R.J.R.	
"	9-5-16	9 a.m. ~11 p.m.	Overhead indirect fire by our Machine Guns on Enemy trenches near A11.a.90.54, also Enemy trench from A17.d.20.22 to A17.d.90.00. — R.J.R.	
"			About 9.30 p.m. a peculiar cloud of smoke or gas was seen to rise from German trenches & float out over our lines. It arose about 150 ft up in the air & no effect was felt. — R.J.R.	

Army Form C. 2118.

WAR DIARY
INTELLIGENCE SUMMARY
(Erase heading not required.)

Instructions regarding War Diaries and Intelligence Summaries are contained in F. S. Regs., Part II. and the Staff Manual respectively. Title Pages will be prepared in manuscript.

Place	Date	Hour	Summary of Events and Information	Remarks and references to Appendices
Trenches				
(ROCLINCOURT 51B N.W. Edition 2C Scale 1:10,000)	10.6.16	6.45pm – 11.15pm	Indirect fire by two of our M. Guns on Enemy Dumps & Trenches near A15 d 36 08, 1000 Rounds — R.J.R.	
"	11.6.16	10pm – 11.30pm	Indirect fire was brought to bear on Enemy Positions, as follows:- Enemy Dumps near A11c 70 81 & Enemy Trenches near A11c 20 54 — R.J.R. Casualties:- Pte. HARPER (no 4348) 2/15 London Regt attached to 179 M.G. Coy. wounded.	
"	12.6.16	10 p m – 12.15 am	Two thousand rounds expended in Indirect fire on following:- Enemy Lines — Guns Posts A17a 20 48; LILLE Road from A17c 20 60 to A11c 56 84; & Light Railway A17 b 30 45	

2449 Wt. W14957/M90 750,000 1/16 J.B.C. & A. Forms/C.2118/12.

WAR DIARY
or
INTELLIGENCE SUMMARY
(Erase heading not required.)

Army Form C. 2118.

Place	Date	Hour	Summary of Events and Information	Remarks and references to Appendices
Trenches (ROUINCOURT Sector) Trench Maps ROUINCOURT 51b. N.W.1 Edition 2C Scale 1:10,000	12.5.16	11.15pm	O.C. Guns left sector received a message from O.C. B. Coy 2/13th LONDON Regt. asking guns in left sector to stand to. All "stood to" doubled, but nothing occurred.	
"	"		In all Gun positions ammunition was checked for S.A. & G. ammunition. Each ammunition was changed & fields refilled where necessary. R.J.R.	
"	13.5.16		Enemy artillery active during the last 24 hours, especially about 6 p.m. & 7 p.m. There was intense trench activity on our right. Intermittent shell fire throughout the night culminating in a bombardment by us at 2.a.m. which lasted for about 20 minutes.	
"	"	9.45pm -11p.m	Indirect fire by two of our M. Guns on Enemy Communication & Support Trenches. — R.J.R.	
"	14.3.16		Very quiet day & night. Great aerial activity on our side, as many as 30 of our aeroplanes being seen at once. No German aeroplanes were seen.	

WAR DIARY

INTELLIGENCE SUMMARY
(Erase heading not required.)

Army Form C. 2118.

Instructions regarding War Diaries and Intelligence Summaries are contained in F.S. Regs., Part II. and the Staff Manual respectively. Title Pages will be prepared in manuscript.

Place	Date	Hour	Summary of Events and Information	Remarks and references to Appendices
Trenches ROCLINCOURT Sheet (Trench Map)	14-5-16	10 p.m. – 11 p.m.	Indirect fire was brought to bear on Enemy Trenches near A19 d 60 30 & Cross Roads, Les Tilleuls, A11 c 95 98. 1000 rounds being expended — R.P.R.	
ROCLINCOURT 51.º N.W.1 Edition 2 C Scale 1:10,000	15-5-16		At 12 mid-day a German working party was noticed on a Haystack at A12 c 30 30 one of our m. guns in FORK REDOUBT with range of 2300ᵗ was brought to bear on their trench with satisfactory results. From telescopic observations two at least of the Enemy were killed	
"		10.5 p.m. 11.50 p.m.	1000 rounds Expended in indirect fire at Path from A12 d 02.22 to the LILLE Road at A12 c 46 78. — R.P.R.	
"	16-5-16	6.50 p.m. – 10.35 p.m.	Indirect fire was brought to bear on supposed German working parties on (1) Road at A19a 42 48 (2) KRAMER TRENCH A16 d 96 99 to A19a 36 94 (3) Road at A16 d 57 62, & A16 b 67 57 — R.P.R.	
"	17-5-16	6.30 p.m. – 2 a.m.	Programme of night firing of previous Evening repeated — R.P.R.	

WAR DIARY or INTELLIGENCE SUMMARY

Army Form C. 2118.

August 1916

Place	Date	Hour	Summary of Events and Information	Remarks and references to Appendices
Trenches	15.8.16	—	Nothing of importance to chronicle — R.J.R.	
ROCLINCOURT Sector French Map ROCLINCOURT 51 B.N.W.1 Edition 2c Scale 1:10,000	19.8.16	9.45 p.m – 11.15 p.m	Indirect fire was brought to bear on enemy dump at A17.90.01 & the road from A17.8.00 to A19.a.5.68. Casualties:- Killed by French trench mortar exploding prematurely Pte J. Nicholls No 25904. — R.J.R.	
"	20.8.16	4 p.m – 12 m.n.	Indirect fire was brought to bear as under:- (1) Path & light railway A12.b.0.2 — A12.c.40.78 (2) L.i.46 Road (A17.a.20.60 — A11.c.50.24) — R.J.R.	
"	21.8.16		Nothing of importance to Chronicle — R.J.R.	

Army Form C. 2118.

WAR DIARY
INTELLIGENCE SUMMARY
(Erase heading not required.)

(a) August 1916

Instructions regarding War Diaries and Intelligence Summaries are contained in F. S. Regs., Part II. and the Staff Manual respectively. Title Pages will be prepared in manuscript.

Place	Date	Hour	Summary of Events and Information	Remarks and references to Appendices
Trenches	22.5.16		Night firing:- Induced fire was brought to bear on the Enemy as follows:-	
ROCLINCOURT (Sheet)			Gun wares at A11 & 60.75 (500 rounds)	
1 French Map			Light railway at A9.9. 30.45 (500 rounds) — Rgh	
ROCLINCOURT			Gun wares LES TILLEULS (A11 a.9.0 60) — R.g.R.	
51st N.W. 1 Edition 2C Scale 1:10,000	23.5.16	—	Nothing of importance to Chronicle — R.g.R.	
	24.5.16		Observation Post commenced in FORK REDOUBT near A11 & 20.35.	
		10 p.m. -12.30 a.m.	1250 rounds expended in Indirect fire on Various points within & behind Enemy lines — R.g.R.	
"			Very quiet day.	
"	25.5.16		1500 rounds expended in Indirect fire on Dumps, & light Railway in hostile area — R.g.R.	

WAR DIARY
INTELLIGENCE SUMMARY

Army Form C. 2118.

Instructions regarding War Diaries and Intelligence Summaries are contained in F.S. Regs., Part II. and the Staff Manual respectively. Title Pages will be prepared in manuscript.

(Erase heading not required.)

Place	Date	Hour	Summary of Events and Information	Remarks and references to Appendices
ROCLINCOURT (Trench map)	26/8/16	9.30pm 11.30pm	2000 rounds were fired in indirect fire on following points viz:— enemy huts :— (i) Cross Roads LES TILLEULS (ii) Sugar Refinery THELUS (A19.a.20.6f) (iii) Junction of Railways A12.a.0.7.6.3 (iv) Road from Arras to La Folie A19.4.5.4.6 — R.J.R.	
ROCLINCOURT 51° N.W.1 Edition 2C Scale 1:10,000	27/8/16	—	Light enemy on Roclincourt spoilt — R.J.R.	
"	27/8/16		Direct fire was brought to bear on the enemy from 6.45 a.m. on THELUS 4 fields in front of Sugar mill, searching for, & making practice. 1700 rounds were fired. About 6 p.m. our position A11.0.9.9.9 was hit by a hostile shell. No casualties were caused, but a good deal of material was damaged. The gun was unharmed — R.J.R.	
"	28/8/16		Quiet day enemy — R.J.R.	

WAR DIARY.

179 Machine Gun Company.

September 1916

① September 1916

Army Form C.2118

WAR DIARY
or
INTELLIGENCE SUMMARY
(Erase heading not required.)

Instructions regarding War Diaries and Intelligence Summaries are contained in F.S. Regs., Part II. and the Staff Manual respectively. Title Pages will be prepared in manuscript.

Place	Date	Hour	Summary of Events and Information	Remarks and references to Appendices
Trenches	30-8-16	—	Nothing of importance to report. Usual Trench Routine. — R.J.R.	
(French Map ROCLINCOURT 51B.N.W.1 Edition 2C Scale 1:10,000)	31-8-16	9.30 p.m. 11 p.m.	Some of our M. Guns carried out Indirect fire on portions of the LILLE Road Ridge, from A11a 90.75 to A11c 50.69 and from A11c 50.69 to A11a 12.60. Expending 1500 rounds. — R.J.R. Enemy M. Guns were active about 10.30 p.m.	
"	1-9-16	9.15 p.m. — 11.45 p.m.	Indirect fire brought to bear on Cross Roads (A5c 11.21), Trenches near A11a 20.54, & Dump A11c 70.61: 1500 rounds. Between 11 a.m. & 11.30 a.m. our Artillery were active & numbers of Shrapnel Shells burst prematurely over our own support line.	
"			Between 6 p.m. & 7 p.m. our support line was shelled by Enemy Artillery. Trench being blown in & much shrapnel damage. — R.J.R.	
"	2-9-16	6 a.m.	One of our M. Guns fired 250 rounds at a German Working Party. The working party dispersed.	

September 1916

Army Form C. 2118

WAR DIARY
or
INTELLIGENCE SUMMARY
(Erase heading not required.)

Instructions regarding War Diaries and Intelligence Summaries are contained in F.S. Regs., Part II. and the Staff Manual respectively. Title Pages will be prepared in manuscript.

Place	Date	Hour	Summary of Events and Information	Remarks and references to Appendices
Trenches 1st French Map	2-9-16	6.45 p.m. 11.15 p.m.	2500 rounds expended on Junction of Light Railways, Light Railway & LILLE Road.	
ROCLINCOURT 51st M.W.I Division 2C Scale 1:10,000			Some Trench Mortars landed close to M. Gun position in support line in Left Batt-Sector between 10 p.m. & 11 p.m. No damage was done. R.J.R.	
"	3-9-16	9 p.m. 10 p.m.	Indirect fire was brought to bear on Cross Roads in THELUS, & Enemy Communication Trenches A16.d.90.24 to A19.c.45.00. Enemy Trench Mortars were active during afternoon & evening. R.J.R.	
"	4-9-16	5.30 a.m. 6 A.M.	200 rounds fired at German working parties S.E. of Mill A6.c.70.95.	
"		9.30 p.m. 11.30 p.m.	Indirect fire was brought to bear various points within & behind Enemy Lines — R.J.R.	

③ Sept. 1916

WAR DIARY
INTELLIGENCE SUMMARY
(Erase heading not required.)

Army Form C. 2118

Instructions regarding War Diaries and Intelligence Summaries are contained in F.S. Regs., Part II. and the Staff Manual respectively. Title Pages will be prepared in manuscript.

Place	Date	Hour	Summary of Events and Information	Remarks and references to Appendices
TRENCHES (Trench Map)	5-9-16	9p.m – 11p.m	Indirect fire was brought to bear on Cross Roads LES TILLEUX & Communication Trench from A9a 25.92 to A11c 60.22. — R.J.R.	
ROCLINCOURT 51B N.W. I Edition 2C Scale 1:10,000	6-9-16		About 10 p.m. shock of mine explosion was felt followed by a heavy bombardment from our Artillery till 11 p.m. — R.J.R.	
"	7-9-16	9.15 p.m – 11p.m	Indirect fire was brought to bear on Paths, Light Railway A12 b 02.22 to A12c 40.98. Junction of Light Railways A15 a 07.63. & Roads and Light Railway A9 a.33.50. We exploded a mine at 3.20 p.m. and a slight bombardment followed — R.J.R.	
"	8-9-16	—	Nothing of importance to chronicle — R.J.R.	

WAR DIARY
INTELLIGENCE SUMMARY
(Erase heading not required.)

Army Form C. 2118

(1) Sept. 1916

Instructions regarding War Diaries and Intelligence Summaries are contained in F. S. Regs., Part II. and the Staff Manual respectively. Title Pages will be prepared in manuscript.

Place	Date	Hour	Summary of Events and Information	Remarks and references to Appendices
Trenches	9-9-16		The day was quiet as a whole. Our heavy artillery shelled enemy trenches	
1" French Map ROCLINCOURT 51.B. N.W.1 Ecurie 2C Scale 1:10,000		6.15 p.m. 11.15 p.m.	Indirect fire was brought to bear on Cross Roads (Ant 65.95) THELUS & trench from Aet 96.05 to Asa 36.21 by two M. Guns — R.R.R.	
"	10-9-16		No 1 Section took part in a successful raid on the right by 2/15th London Regiment. Two guns were in the front line in PARIS REDOUBT. The left hand gun was for emergencies & did not fire. The right hand gun fired a barrage fire across "No Man's" Land & fired between 3 & 3.30 a.m. superimposing 2,500 rounds. Two support guns fired short bursts from 3.15 a.m. to 3.25 a.m. to guide Raiders returning. — R.R.R.	
"	11-9-16	12.30 a.m. 3 a.m.	Two of our M. Guns fired 3000 rounds (indirect fire) at KRAMER WEG between points Ant 61.22 & Asc 99.48. — R.R.R.	
"	12-9-16	—	Quiet day & night — R.R.R.	

Sept. 1916

Army Form C. 2118

WAR DIARY
-or-
INTELLIGENCE SUMMARY
(Erase heading not required.)

Instructions regarding War Diaries and Intelligence Summaries are contained in F.S. Regs., Part II. and the Staff Manual respectively. Title Pages will be prepared in manuscript.

Place	Date	Hour	Summary of Events and Information	Remarks and references to Appendices
Trenches	13-9-16	—	Another quiet and uneventful day — R.J.R.	
Trench Map 14-9-16			Considerable shelling by both sides throughout the day	
ROCLINCOURT 51.B.N.W.1 Edition 2.C Scale 1:10,000		9.15 p.m. 11.30 p.m	Indirect fire by two of our M. Guns on Cross Roads (A11.c 60.75) THÉLUS & Communication Trench A11.c 76.05 to A.5.a 36.21 — R.J.R.	
"	15-9-16		The day and night were on the whole quiet.	
		9 p.m 11 p.m	Two of our M. Guns carried out indirect fire on Enemy Communication Trenches — R.J.R.	
"	16-9-16		Between 10 p.m & 10.30 p.m. some heavy Enemy shells fell near our support line.	
		9.10 p.m 11 p.m	Indirect fire was brought to bear on Cross Roads & Communication Trench in Enemy area — R.J.R.	
"	17-9-16	—	Nothing of importance to chronicle — R.J.R.	

September 1916

WAR DIARY
INTELLIGENCE SUMMARY
(Erase heading not required.)

Army Form C. 2118

Instructions regarding War Diaries and Intelligence Summaries are contained in F.S. Regs., Part II. and the Staff Manual respectively. Title Pages will be prepared in manuscript.

Place	Date	Hour	Summary of Events and Information	Remarks and references to Appendices
Trenches	19-9-16	10.10 p.m.	Indirect fire was brought to bear by two G. over M. Guns on Enemy Dumps &	
Tosquin M.G/S		11.25 p.m.	Road (A11c 00.72 to A11a 90.65) — R.J.R.	
ROUNCOURT	19-9-16	—	Quiet day on our Brigade front — R.J.R.	
51.B N.W.1				
Edition 2.C	20-9-16	6.50 p.m.	Indirect fire was brought to bear by two G. over M. Guns on Enemy Communication	
(Scale 1:10,000)		10 p.m.	Trench, Light Railway Junction, and LILLE Road from A11a 90.65 to A11c 56.84 — R.J.R.	
"	21-9-16	—	On the whole a quiet day — R.J.R.	
"	22-9-16	9.30 p.m.	Indirect fire by two G. over M. Guns on LILLE Road (A17a 12.61 to A16d 05.90),	
		10.45 p.m.	Enemy Communication Trench & Dumps. — R.J.R.	
"	23-9-16		During a successful Raid by 2/16 London Regt at 11 p.m. on German Trenches near the PULPIT Crater one Gun Team took part in the operations as follows:— on the right flank of the ending party a barrage fire was maintained from Sap 43c to the German Trenches at about A10.b 35.65 from 11 p.m. to 11.25 p.m. 1000 rounds were fired — R.J.R.	

WAR DIARY
INTELLIGENCE SUMMARY
(Erase heading not required.)

Army Form C. 2118

Sept. 1916

Instructions regarding War Diaries and Intelligence Summaries are contained in F.S. Regs., Part II. and the Staff Manual respectively. Title Pages will be prepared in manuscript.

Place	Date	Hour	Summary of Events and Information	Remarks and references to Appendices
Trench Map BELINCOURT 57B N.W.I	24-9-16	7.45pm – 8pm	Indirect fire by two of our M. Guns on Enemy Light Railway, Roads THEIVS, & German H.Q. near Sq.d 50.60 – – R.J.R.	
Estrée 2C Scale 1:12,000	25-9-16	–	Nothing of importance to report – – R.J.R.	
	26-9-16	–	Indirect fire was carried out by two of our M. Guns on two portions of the LILLE Road – – R.J.R.	
"	27-9-16	–	Nothing of importance to chronicle. R.J.R.	
"	28-9-16	7.30pm – 10.30pm	The day has quiet on the whole. Indirect fire was brought to bear on the following points:— Road & Light Railway, Communication Trench, & Roads in THEIVS. R.J.R.	

Sept 1916

WAR DIARY
INTELLIGENCE SUMMARY
(Erase heading not required.)

Army Form C. 2

Place	Date	Hour	Summary of Events and Information	Remarks and references to Appendices
Trenches Trench Map ROCLINCOURT 51B N.W.1 Edition 2C Scale 1:10000	24-9-16		1500 rounds were fired from a point near the BERNE salient east of BENTATA Sap in support of the raid by 2/14 th LONDON Regt. Fire was opened as directed, but had to cease earlier than intended owing to the breakage of a muzzle cap. — R.J.R.	
"			Considerable difficulty has been experienced in keeping the Transport of the Coy. up to efficiency. This difficulty arises from the number of men allotted to the Coy. as Drivers. By the present Establishment a M.G. Coy is allowed only 22 men & 1 Sergt. to look after 43 mules, 10 horses, 12 limbers, 8 light carts, 4 lorries. This number of Drivers is the bare workable minimum under peace conditions. On active service this number of Drivers is found to be insufficient. Being a bare minimum it does not allow for certain contingencies: e.g. one man going sick necessitates one of the other Drivers having to work after two additional animals, which he cannot do properly. At present we have 4 Drivers in Hospital. The result being that every other Driver has 3 animals to look after. There is, too, behind the Trenches the constant necessity for making standings and improving stables for the animals, & as Pioneer help is not, in fact seldom, is available, the Drivers have this work to do in addition to their ordinary stable duties. On active service animals need, if anything, more attention than under peace conditions at home. Two or three animals sick may seriously jeopardise the efficiency & mobility of the Transport and consequently of the whole Coy. And further the present Personnel of A.D.S.S./Forms/C.2118. of Drivers is almost impossible to keep animals fit & in good condition. — R.J.R.	

Vol 5

Secret

WAR DIARY
of
179th Machine Gun Company
from
1st October 1916 to 31st October 1916.

Vol 5

Secret

WAR DIARY

of

179th Machine Gun Company

from

1st October 1916 to 31st October 1916.

October 1916

WAR DIARY
INTELLIGENCE SUMMARY

Army Form C. 2118

Instructions regarding War Diaries and Intelligence Summaries are contained in F.S. Regs., Part II. and the Staff Manual respectively. Title Pages will be prepared in manuscript.

(Erase heading not required.)

Place	Date	Hour	Summary of Events and Information	Remarks and references to Appendices
Trenches	29-9-16	—	Nothing of importance to report. R.J.R.	
BOUZINCOURT Map M.W.1 S.E. Edition 2c Scale 1/10,000	30-9-16		In accordance with orders received here of our M.Guns were mounted in the Front Line, Pickard Ave 95.15 and Ave 59.38. From each of these positions fire was opened on Enemy's support line where it had been cut by our Artillery, at 9.30 p.m. 11.0 p.m. & 12.30 a.m. 750 rounds being fired each time from each gun. Total 4,500 rounds. On fire being opened the Enemy sent up a red light but no return fire was seen. There was some reply with Torpedoes & mortars, but no damage was done. R.J.R.	
"	1-10-16	9 p.m. to 9.30 p.m.	2,000 rounds expended in indirect fire on Enemy Communication Trenches & Junction of Trenches. All guns were ready at 5.45 a.m. for German aircraft. R.J.R.	
"	2-10-16		Three German aeroplanes flew low over the Enemy lines & our Front Line in the morning. All our M.Guns engaged them & two were driven off. The third flew over the lines until 10 a.m. No. of rounds fired 10,800. One Gun was apparently broken & several Chinese Wonder fired aircraft at it. R.J.R.	

October 1916

WAR DIARY
INTELLIGENCE SUMMARY
(Erase heading not required.)

Army Form C. 2118

Instructions regarding War Diaries and Intelligence Summaries are contained in F.S. Regs., Part II. and the Staff Manual respectively. Title Pages will be prepared in manuscript.

Place	Date	Hour	Summary of Events and Information	Remarks and references to Appendices
Trenches	3-10-16	5.30 p.m.	Enemy aeroplane appeared & was engaged by M.G's. Several grand & field artillery. It was not apparently damaged however.	
ROCLINCOURT Map. H.W.1 51st Edition 2c. Scale 1/10,000		7 p.m. 9 p.m.	Indirect fire was carried out by our M.G's on Paths & Light Railway in enemy area. — R.J.R.	
"	4-10-16	7 p.m. 8.30 p.m.	1750 rounds expended in indirect fire on LILLE ROAD Aue 90.75 — Auc 56.84 and Cross Roads A9c 10.48. — R.J.R.	
"	5-10-16		Two of our M.G's working in co-operation with the Centre Bgy. 2/15th London Regt were moved up to the front line near where the trench was knocked in by shell fire in case of hostile raid. Indirect fire was carried out as usual on hostile area. — R.J.R.	
"	6-10-16	7 p.m. — 9 p.m. 6.45 p.m. — 8.20 p.m.	Nothing of importance to report. Usual indirect fire operations on Dump Auc 70.21 and Cross Roads THEIR A12c 55.81 and Light Railway A12 t 0.22 to A12c 40.95 — R.J.R.	

(B) October 1916

WAR DIARY
— or —
INTELLIGENCE SUMMARY
(Erase heading not required.)

Army Form C. 2118

Instructions regarding War Diaries and Intelligence Summaries are contained in F. S. Regs., Part II. and the Staff Manual respectively. Title Pages will be prepared in manuscript.

Place	Date	Hour	Summary of Events and Information	Remarks and references to Appendices
Trenches	7-10-16	—	Nothing of importance to report. R.J.R.	
(ROCLINCOURT pap. 51.B. N.W.1 Edition 2c. Scale 1/10,000)	8-10-16	6:24 p.m —	1950 rounds expended in Indirect fire on Roads & Light Rys., & Junctions of Roads & Light Ry. in Izabels area — R.J.R.	
	9-10-16	9:10 p.m 9 p.m — 10 p.m	Issued Indirect fire operations on Cross Roads in Izabels area — R.J.R.	
"	10-10-16	1:10 p.m	A German working party was observed near point A11.20.15 and was fired at by one 3" mor M.G. from FORK Redoubt. One belt dispersed this party.	
"	"	5:20 p.m —10:15 p.m	2500 rounds were expended in Indirect fire on Cross Roads A.S.C. 11.21 & LILLE Road from A.12.c.15.60 to A.11.c 56.95. In anticipation of an expected raid by the Enemy all overhead guns opened to thicken the night with Barrage fire laid on the Enemy Support line. — R.J.R.	
"	11-10-16		Nothing of importance to report. The usual Indirect fire of previous three carried out by two of our M.G's. 2090 rounds being expended. — R.J.R	

(4) October 1916

Army Form C. 2118

WAR DIARY
or
INTELLIGENCE SUMMARY
(Erase heading not required.)

Instructions regarding War Diaries and Intelligence Summaries are contained in F. S. Regs., Part II. and the Staff Manual respectively. Title Pages will be prepared in manuscript.

Place	Date	Hour	Summary of Events and Information	Remarks and references to Appendices
Trenches	12-10-16	7 p.m.	Indirect fire operations will carried out Targets being as follows :-	
ROCLINCOURT		10 p.m.	(1) LILLE Road Anc 90.75 to Anc 56.64	
Map 51.N.W.1			(2) LILLE Road Anc 90.75 to Anc 65.64 by 2nd Gun.	
Edition 2c			(3) Dump Anc 70.81	
Scale 1/20,000			2000 rounds were fired — R.J.R.	
"	13-10-16	—	Nothing of importance to report — R.J.R.	
"	14-10-16	7 p.m. – 9 p.m.	Usual indirect fire operations carried out R.J.R	
"	15-10-16	—	Nothing of importance to report — R.J.R.	
"	16-10-16	—	Rifle firing carried out as usual - R.J.R	
"	17-10-16		Indirect fire was brought to bear on Enemy as under :-	
			(1) 750 rounds on Road Anc 90.90 to Ash 30.64 between 7 p.m & 7.58 p.m.	
			(2) 750 rounds on LILLE Road from Anc 60.75 to Anc 56.84, between 9.16 p.m & 9.20 p.m. R.J.R.	

(5) October 1916

WAR DIARY
INTELLIGENCE SUMMARY
(Erase heading not required.)

Army Form C. 2118

Instructions regarding War Diaries and Intelligence Summaries are contained in F.S. Regs., Part II. and the Staff Manual respectively. Title Pages will be prepared in manuscript.

Place	Date	Hour	Summary of Events and Information	Remarks and references to Appendices
Trenches	18-10-16		Enemy positions were searched by Indirect fire as follows:—	
FONCQUEVILLERS Map 57.D. N.W.1 Edition 2.C. Scale 1/10,000	19-10-16		(1) 500 rounds at Light Ry. A12.B.02.22 to A12.B.40.95, between 6.45 p.m. & 7.30 p.m. (2) 500 rounds at Cross Roads THEUS A12.C.20.68, between 7.35 p.m. & 8.0 p.m. (3) 1750 rounds at Cross Roads A17.a.10.46, between 7.5 p.m. & 8.20 p.m. — R.J.R. Light firing operations carried out as usual — R.J.R.	
"	20-10-16		Nothing of importance to report. R.J.R.	
"	21-10-16	8.30 a.m.	Enemy aeroplane observed flying low over our lines, over M.G. in FORK Redoubt fired at same. R.J.R.	
"	22-10-16		One of our M.G's in Support Line was discharged by enemy minenwerfer. No casualties. — R.J.R.	
"	23-10-16	—	Nothing of importance to chronicle — R.J.R.	

October 1916

WAR DIARY
INTELLIGENCE SUMMARY
(Erase heading not required.)

Army Form C. 2118

Instructions regarding War Diaries and Intelligence Summaries are contained in F.S. Regs., Part II. and the Staff Manual respectively. Title Pages will be prepared in manuscript.

Place	Date	Hour	Summary of Events and Information	Remarks and references to Appendices
Trenches	24-10-16	—	Nothing of importance to report. R.J.R.	
Roclincourt Map 51.B.N.W.1 Edition 2C Scale 1/10,000	25-10-16		Company relieved by 9th Canadian M.G. Coy. Relief completed by 11 p.m. — R.J.R.	
	26-10-16		Company marched from BRAY at 2 p.m. Travelling via ECOIVRES, ACQ, HAUTE-AVESNES, HERMAVILLE arriving at TILLOY-LES-HERMAVILLE about 5 p.m. & was billeted there for the night. — R.J.R.	
	27-10-16	9 a.m.	Left TILLOY-LES-HERMAVILLE & went on to IZEL-LES-HAMEAU, VILLERS-SIRE-SIMON, AMBRINES, MAGNICOURT, HOUVIN, MONCHEAUX arriving at BUNEVILLE about 2.30 p.m. where company went into billets for two nights. R.J.R.	
	29-10-16	6.15 a.m.	Company left BUNEVILLE and marched via FRÉVENT, PROUVILLE, BEAUMETZ to RIBEAUCOURT where it was billeted — R.J.R.	
RIBEAUCOURT	30-10-16 31-10-16	— —	Usual company parades — R.J.R.	

Vol 6

Confidential

War Diary

of

119th Machine Gun Co

for

November 1st - 30th 1916

November 1916

Army Form C. 2118

WAR DIARY
INTELLIGENCE SUMMARY
(Erase heading not required.)

Instructions regarding War Diaries and Intelligence Summaries are contained in F. S. Regs., Part II. and the Staff Manual respectively. Title Pages will be prepared in manuscript.

Place	Date	Hour	Summary of Events and Information	Remarks and references to Appendices
RIBEAUCOURT	1/11/16	—	Company in Billets. — R.J.R.	
"	2/11/16	—	26 men attached to the Company from 4 Battalions in Brigade — R.J.R.	
"	3/11/16	—	Company leaves RIBEAUCOURT for VAUCHELLES-LES-QUESNOY passing through following places en route :— FRANCU, GORENFLOS, ERGINES, AILLY-LE-HAUT-CLOCHER, & BUGNY-L'ABBÉ.	
VAUCHELLES-LES-QUESNOY	4/11/16	—	Usual Company parades — R.J.R.	
"	5/11/16	—	Church parades, followed by Company Drill — R.J.R.	
"	6/11/16	—	All wheeled transport (with the exception of water cart & cooks cart) & all animals (with exception of 10 Officers' chargers & 3 mules) handed over to A.S.C. — R.J.R.	
"	7/11/16	—	Usual Company parades — R.J.R.	
"	8/11/16	—	" " " — R.J.R.	
"	9/11/16	—	" " " — R.J.R.	
"	10/11/16	—	" " " — R.J.R.	

November 1916

Army Form C. 2118

WAR DIARY
INTELLIGENCE SUMMARY
(Erase heading not required.)

Instructions regarding War Diaries and Intelligence Summaries are contained in F.S. Regs., Part II. and the Staff Manual respectively. Title Pages will be prepared in manuscript.

Place	Date	Hour	Summary of Events and Information	Remarks and references to Appendices
VAUCHELLES-lès-QUESNOY	11/11/16	—	Tactical defense scheme of BELLANCOURT carried out by the Company — R.J.R.	
"	12/11/16	—	Church Parade in the morning. Gym held in the afternoon — R.J.R.	
"	13/11/16	—	Company Parade — R.J.R.	
"	14/11/16	—	" " — R.J.R.	
"	15/11/16	—	" " — R.J.R.	
"	16/11/16	—	3 mules & remainder of wheeled Transport (less Cooks' Cart & Water Cart) handed over to A.S.C. — R.J.R.	
"	19/11/16	—	11 p.m. Company leaves VAUCHELLES-LÈS-QUESNOY for entrainment at LONGPRÉ — R.J.R.	
In train	19/11/16	10 a.m.	Left LONGPRÉ en route for MARSEILLES — R.J.R.	
"	19/11/16	—	En route.	
"	20/11/16	5.30 p.m	Train arrives at MARSEILLES Company marches to CENTI Camp — R.J.R.	
Camp	21/11/16	—	In Camp (at CENTI) MARSEILLES — R.J.R.	
"	22/11/16	—	" " — R.J.R.	

Army Form C. 2118

WAR DIARY
INTELLIGENCE SUMMARY
(Erase heading not required.)

November 1916

Place	Date	Hour	Summary of Events and Information	Remarks and references to Appendices
In Camp at MARSEILLES	23/11/16	—	Usual Company parades — R.J.R.	
"	24/11/16	—	" — R.J.R.	
"	25/11/16	—	Company leaves Camp at 10 a.m. and Embarks on H.M.T. CALEDONIA. Ship leaves port at 11 p.m. 4.7 m.m. Gun are mounted on Boat deck and 4" in the bow — R.J.R.	
At Sea	26/11/16	—	10 Officers changed follow on H.M.T. CALEDONIAN. Company parades for Physical drill, etc — R.J.R.	
"	27/11/16	—	" — R.J.R.	
"	28/11/16	—	" — R.J.R.	
"	29/11/16	—	" — R.J.R.	
"	30/11/16	—	" — R.J.R.	
"	1/12/16	—	Ship is wharfed at SALONIKA. Disembarkation commences at 12.45 p.m. Company marches from Docks at 2 p.m. and arrives in Camp 5 miles beyond Town of SALONIKA at 5 p.m. — R.J.R.	

R. Rogers Lieut.
for Major Commanding
179 M.G.C.

www.ingramcontent.com/pod-product-compliance
Lightning Source LLC
Chambersburg PA
CBHW081457160426
43193CB00013B/2508